55 Mujjious

55 Muffins

Tried and True

PENGUIN BOOKS

PENGUIN BOOKS
Penguin Books (NZ) Ltd, cnr Airborne and Rosedale Roads, Albany, Auckland 1310, New Zealand
Penguin Books Ltd, 27 Wrights Lane, London W8 5TZ, England
Penguin Putnam Inc, 375 Hudson Street, New York, NY 10014, United States
Penguin Books Australia Ltd, 487 Maroondah Highway, Ringwood, Australia 3134
Penguin Books Canada Ltd, 10 Alcorn Avenue, Toronto, Ontario, Canada M4V 3B2
Penguin Books (South Africa) Pty Ltd, 5 Watkins Street, Denver Ext 4, 2094, South Africa
Penguin Books India (P) Ltd, 11, Community Centre, Panchsheel Park, New Delhi 110 017, India
Penguin Books Ltd, Registered Offices: Harmondsworth, Middlesex, England

First published as *Granny's Muffins* by Penguin Books (NZ) Ltd, 1993

1 3 5 7 9 10 8 6 4 2

Copyright © Penguin Books, 2000
The right of Penguin Books to be identified as the author of this work in terms of section 96 of the
Copyright Act 1994 is hereby asserted.

Front cover photograph: Zucchini & Wheatgerm Muffins and Cheese & Lentil Muffins
Back cover photograph: Plum Muffin

Designed and typeset by Flip Publishing
Printed in Australia by Australian Print Group, Maryborough

All rights reserved. Without limiting the rights under copyright reserved above, no part of this
publication may be reproduced, stored in or introduced into a retrieval system, or transmitted,
in any form or by any means (electronic, mechanical, photocopying, recording or otherwise),
without the prior written permission of both the copyright owner and the above
publisher of this book.

Contents

Introduction..6

Hints for Making the Best Muffins..7

Savoury Muffins..8

Sweet Muffins..23

Spicy Muffins..57

Index..63

Introduction

Close your eyes and imagine being surrounded by a fog of freshly baked muffin smells. You sit down in the sunroom with a hot cup of tea or coffee, those still-warm muffins, and a large dish of butter ...

These are the joys of muffin baking and muffin eating. Muffins are so special because they are easy to make, are versatile, and smell and taste great. They can be matched with any meal, and they make a healthy snack.

This book contains 55 favourite recipes. They have been divided into three categories: savoury, sweet and spicy muffins. All are found in alphabetical order in the index.

Muffins freeze well so any extras can be put away for another day. But as they are so easy to bake, why not have them fresh?

It is easy to adapt the recipes and make up new combinations. By following the hints for great muffins that follow, you can have hours of delicious fun trying out new ideas.

We hope you enjoy the recipes in this book, and your own creations.

Happy eating.

Hints for Making the Best Muffins

*T*here are many useful tips for improving the taste and texture of your muffins but they will all be to no avail if you overmix your batter – tough muffins can be a tough lesson. You should mix just enough to combine the wet and dry ingredients.

Pre-heat the oven to the required temperature and grease the muffin pans before you start. Also, have a read through the recipe before you begin so that you have all the chopping, grating and blending done before you start mixing the ingredients. The less time spent mixing things together, the better. Too much liquid in the mixture will result in soggy and flat muffins. Too little liquid and they'll end up hard and dry. Also, white flour instead of wholemeal will give you a lighter muffin.

Bake the muffins in the middle of the oven, and be adaptable with the temperature and timing of cooking – every oven behaves differently. The oven is too hot if the muffin tops are uneven and cracked, and it is too cool if the tops are pale and have not risen.

If microwaving bran muffins, mix oil and bran first, then mix it with the rest of the ingredients. This will result in a more moist muffin. When you take the muffins out of the oven, leave them to stand for two or three minutes.

To re-heat muffins, wrap them loosely in aluminium foil and put in the oven for five to ten minutes at 125°C, or 15 to 20 minutes at 180°C if they are frozen.

SAVOURY MUFFINS

Bacon & Cheese Muffins

Great in the winter with fresh tomato soup.

1 cup flour
½ teaspoon salt
1 teaspoon baking powder
1½ cups bran
¼ cup sugar
½ teaspoon baking soda
1½ cups milk
1 tablespoon butter, melted
1 egg, lightly beaten
1 tablespoon golden syrup
3 rashers cooked bacon
1 cup grated tasty cheese

SIFT flour, salt and baking powder. Stir in bran and sugar, and make a well in the centre. Dissolve baking soda in milk. Beat egg lightly. Combine milk, melted butter, egg and golden syrup. Add chopped bacon and cheese to dry ingredients, then pour in the milk mixture. Stir until just combined. Three-quarters fill greased muffin pans and bake at 200°C for 10-15 minutes.

Bacon & Tomato Muffins

Try these with a thin cream cheese spread.

2 cups flour
1 tablespoon baking powder
4 rashers bacon
2 tomatoes
2 tablespoons tomato concentrate
1 egg
3/4 cup milk
50g butter, melted

SIFT flour and baking powder. Cut rind off bacon and chop flesh. Skin and de-seed tomatoes, and chop roughly. Mix bacon, tomatoes, tomato concentrate, egg and milk together. Pour tomato mixture and melted butter onto dry ingredients. Stir until just combined. Three-quarters fill greased muffin pans and bake at 200°C for 15-20 minutes.

Bean Sprout & Cottage Cheese Muffins

Favourite of the health food fans.

2 cups flour
4 teaspoons baking powder
½ teaspoon salt
¼ teaspoon white pepper
1 teaspoon curry powder
1½ cups unprocessed bran
100g butter
2 cups bean sprouts
1 egg
1¼ cups milk
1 cup cottage cheese with chives

SIFT flour, baking powder, salt, white pepper and curry powder. Stir in bran. Cut in butter until mixture resembles coarse breadcrumbs. Add bean sprouts. Make a well in centre of dry ingredients. Lightly beat egg and milk together. Add to dry ingredients. Stir until just combined. Fold in cottage cheese. Three-quarters fill greased muffin pans and bake at 200ºC for 15-20 minutes.

Caraway & Cheese Muffins

The caraway seeds give these muffins a unique and delicious flavour.

2 cups flour
1 tablespoon baking powder
1/4 teaspoon salt
1 teaspoon dried mustard
1 cup grated cheese
1 tablespoon caraway seeds
1 egg
3/4 cup milk
50g butter, melted

SIFT flour, baking powder and salt. Stir in mustard, grated cheese and caraway seeds. Combine egg and milk. Stir egg and milk and melted butter into dry ingredients until just combined. Three-quarters fill greased muffin pans and bake at 200ºC for 15-20 minutes.

SAVOURY MUFFINS

Carrot Muffins

A morning tea favourite.

2 cups flour
4 teaspoons baking powder
1 cup grated cheese
1 grated onion
1 cup grated carrots
chopped parsley
2 tablespoons bacon bits
1 egg
1 large tablespoon butter, melted
1 cup milk

SIFT flour and baking powder. Add cheese, onion, carrot, parsley and bacon bits. Beat egg; add melted butter and milk. Mix all until just combined. Three-quarters fill greased muffin pans and bake at 200°C for 15-20 minutes.

SAVOURY MUFFINS

Cheese Muffins

One of the originals and one of the best.

2 cups flour
3 teaspoons baking powder
¼ teaspoon salt
½ teaspoon dry mustard
freshly ground black pepper
2 cups grated tasty cheese
2 eggs
1 cup milk

SIFT flour, baking powder, salt, mustard, and freshly ground pepper. Add grated cheese. Lightly beat eggs and milk together. Add eggs and milk to the dry ingredients and mix together lightly until just combined. Three-quarters fill greased muffin pans and bake at 200°C for 10-15 minutes or until golden brown.

SAVOURY MUFFINS

Cheese & Lentil Muffins

A special treat at lunchtime.

1 cup grated tasty cheese
1 cup cooked lentils
1 cup flour
2 teaspoons baking powder
¼ teaspoon salt
1 teaspoon dry mustard
freshly ground black pepper
1 egg
½ cup milk
sesame seeds for sprinkling

COMBINE cheese and lentils. Sift flour, baking powder, salt, mustard and pepper. Add cheese and lentils. Lightly beat egg and milk. Stir into dry ingredients until just combined. Three-quarters fill greased muffin pans and sprinkle sesame seeds over muffins. Bake at 200°C for 15-20 minutes.

ID
Cheese & Onion Muffins

Wonderful with thick vegetable soup.

$1/2$ cup chopped onion
1 tablespoon melted butter
1 egg, lightly beaten
$1/2$ cup milk
$1 1/2$ cups self-raising flour
pinch salt
1 level tablespoon butter
1 cup grated tasty cheese
1 tablespoon poppy seeds
1 tablespoon melted butter for drizzling

COOK onion in one tablespoon of melted butter until lightly brown. Mix beaten egg and milk together. Sift flour and salt. Rub in one tablespoon of butter. Mix dry ingredients with egg and milk to make a light scone batter. Add onion and half the cheese. Place small rounds in greased muffin pans and sprinkle with grated cheese and poppy seeds. Drizzle melted butter over top of muffins. Bake at 220°C for 15 minutes or until cooked.

SAVOURY MUFFINS

Cheesy Sunflower Seed Muffins

Surprise packages in your favourite cheese muffins.

2 cups self-raising flour
1/4 teaspoon salt
1/4 cup butter
1 cup grated tasty cheese
2 teaspoons sunflower seeds
1 egg
1 cup milk
paprika for sprinkling

SIFT flour and salt. Rub in butter until mixture resembles coarse crumbs. Add cheese and sunflower seeds. Beat egg and combine with milk, then add to mixture. Stir until just combined. Three-quarters fill greased muffin pans and sprinkle tops of muffins with paprika. Bake at 200°C for 20-25 minutes.

Chicken & Curry Muffins

A delicious hint of the East.

1¼ cups flour
1 tablespoon baking powder
1 teaspoon curry powder
70g packet chicken soup
¾ cup milk
1 egg
50g butter, melted

SIFT flour, baking powder and curry powder; add soup mix. Combine milk and egg. Melt butter. Make a well in the centre of the dry ingredients. Pour in milk mixture and butter. Stir quickly until just combined. Three-quarters fill greased muffin pans and bake at 200°C for 15-20 minutes.

SAVOURY MUFFINS

Chilli Corn Muffins

A special treat from south of the border.

*1 finely chopped chilli
or 1 teaspoon chilli powder
1 finely chopped small onion
$1/4$ cup cooking oil
$1^{1}/_{2}$ cups All-bran
$1^{1}/_{2}$ cups skim milk
2 egg whites
$1^{2}/_{3}$ cups self-raising flour
1 x 325g can corn kernels, drained
$1/2$ cup tasty cheese
1 egg white, stiffly beaten*

SAUTÉ chilli and onion in one tablespoon of oil until onion is tender. Cool. Place All-bran and milk in a bowl and stand for five minutes to soften. Stir in chilli mixture, remaining oil and two egg whites. Add flour, corn and $1/4$ cup cheese. Finally, fold in remaining stiffly beaten egg white. Three-quarters fill greased muffin pans and sprinkle each muffin with a little of the remaining cheese. Bake at 190ºC for 25-30 minutes.

SAVOURY MUFFINS

Corn & Pecan Muffins

Excellent with pumpkin soup in winter.

3½ cups wholemeal flour
1 cup yellow cornmeal
1 sachet dry yeast
1 teaspoon baking powder
1 teaspoon salt
1 cup milk
100g butter
½ cup water
⅓ cup honey
2 eggs
1 cup chopped pecans
½ cup sultanas

COMBINE one cup flour, cornmeal, yeast, baking powder and salt in a bowl. Heat milk, butter (cut up), water and honey to lukewarm. Beat eggs. Pour liquid and eggs over dry ingredients. Add nuts and sultanas and mix well. Knead on a board for a few minutes. Half fill greased muffin pans and leave in a warm place to rise. Bake at 200°C for 15-18 minutes or until firm.

Savoury Cottage Cheese Muffins

A snack-lover's dream come true.

2 cups flour
½ teaspoon salt
1 teaspoon dry mustard
2½ teaspoons baking powder
25g butter
1 egg
¾ cup milk
250g cottage cheese
¼ cup chopped parsley
1 small onion, finely chopped
¼ cup grated tasty cheese
¼ teaspoon paprika

SIFT flour, salt, mustard and baking powder. Rub in butter. Beat together egg and milk, then add cottage cheese, parsley and onion. Mix well. Stir liquid into dry ingredients until just combined. Three-quarters fill greased muffin pans, then sprinkle mixed grated cheese and paprika over muffins. Bake at 200ºC for 20 minutes. Serve warm.

SAVOURY MUFFINS

Wholemeal Muffins

A classic muffin that is the best.

1 cup milk
1 egg, lightly beaten
2 cups wholemeal self-raising flour
¼ cup raw sugar
½ cup sultanas
100g butter, melted

MIX milk and lightly beaten egg. Combine other ingredients and add liquid mixture. Mix until just combined. Three-quarters fill greased muffin pans and bake at 190°C for 15-20 minutes.

SAVOURY MUFFINS

Zucchini & Wheatgerm Muffins

A delicious complement to most soups.

2 cups flour
1/2 cup wheatgerm
3 teaspoons baking powder
pinch salt
1/2 cup brown sugar
1 cup zucchini, grated
1 egg
1/4 cup oil
3/4 cup milk

COMBINE flour, wheatgerm, baking powder and salt in a bowl. Stir in sugar and zucchini. Beat egg, oil and milk together and stir into mixture until just combined. Three-quarters fill greased muffin pans and bake at 190°C for 20-25 minutes.

# Almond Chip Muffins

Put some crunch in your lunch.

1 3/4 cups self-raising flour
2-3 tablespoons castor sugar
1 teaspoon baking powder
1/2 teaspoon salt
1 egg
3/4 cup milk
1/3 cup butter, melted
2 teaspoons grated lemon peel
1/2 teaspoon vanilla
3/4 cup chopped, unblanched almonds

IN a large bowl, sift together flour, sugar, baking powder and salt. In a small bowl, combine egg, milk, melted butter, grated lemon peel, vanilla and almonds. Add to flour mixture. With a fork, stir briskly until all dry ingredients are just moistened. Batter should look lumpy. Three-quarters fill greased muffin pans and bake at 200°C for 20-25 minutes or until golden brown.

SWEET MUFFINS

Apple Muffins

Another original and still a winner.

1/3 cup vegetable oil
3/4 cup firmly packed brown sugar
1 tablespoon liquid honey
2 eggs, lightly beaten
1 cup grated apple
1/2 cup apple juice
1 1/2 cups All-bran
1 cup wholemeal flour
1/2 cup plain flour
1 1/2 teaspoons baking powder
1/2 cup buttermilk

MIX oil, brown sugar and honey. Add lightly beaten eggs and beat until thoroughly combined. Add grated apple and apple juice. Stir in All-bran. Sift dry ingredients. Stir into egg mixture with buttermilk until just combined. Three-quarters fill greased muffin pans and bake at 220°C for 15 minutes or until firm.

SWEET MUFFINS

Apple, Carrot & Bran Muffins

Mix and match for divine results.

2 eggs, lightly beaten
1/2 cup brown sugar
1/4 cup sunflower oil
2 cups skim milk
1 cup grated carrot
1 cup grated green apple
1 cup raisins
1/2 teaspoon cinnamon
1 cup bran
2 cups flour
1/2 cup wheatgerm
2 teaspoons baking soda
2 teaspoons baking powder

BEAT eggs lightly. Add sugar, oil, milk, carrot, apple and raisins, and stir to mix. Combine rest of ingredients and stir in egg mixture. Cover and chill for at least one hour. Three-quarters fill greased muffin pans and bake at 190ºC for 20 minutes.

Apple, Date & Bran Muffins

Another arrangement of the best ingredients.

2 eggs, lightly beaten
½ cup brown sugar
¼ cup sunflower oil
2 cups skim milk
1 cup chopped dates
1 cup raisins
1 cup grated green apple
½ teaspoon cinnamon
1 cup bran
2 cups flour
½ cup wheatgerm
2 teaspoons baking soda
2 teaspoons baking powder

BEAT eggs lightly. Add sugar, oil, milk, dates and raisins, and stir to mix. Combine rest of ingredients and stir in egg mixture. Cover and chill for at least one hour. Three-quarters fill greased muffin pans and bake at 190°C for 20 minutes or until firm.

Apricot & Lemon Muffins

Refreshing and very moreish.

1 cup flour
½ teaspoon salt
1 teaspoon baking powder
1½ cups bran
¼ cup sugar
½ cup chopped apricots
2 teaspoons grated lemon rind
½ teaspoon baking soda
1 cup milk
1 tablespoon butter, melted
1 egg
1 tablespoon golden syrup

SIFT flour, salt and baking powder. Stir in bran, sugar, chopped apricots and grated lemon rind. Make a well in the centre of dry ingredients. Dissolve baking soda in milk and melt butter. Beat egg lightly. Combine milk, butter, egg and golden syrup, and pour onto dry ingredients. Stir to just combine. Three-quarters fill greased muffin pans and bake at 200°C for 10-15 minutes or until firm.

SWEET MUFFINS

Apricot & Walnut Muffins

Fruit, nuts and a hint of brandy – perfect!

12 dried apricots
2 tablespoons brandy
2 cups flour
1 tablespoon baking powder
½ cup sugar
½ cup chopped walnuts
1 egg
½ cup milk
50g butter, melted

COOK apricots in brandy for five minutes and then roughly chop. Sift flour and baking powder and stir in the sugar, chopped apricots and chopped walnuts. Combine egg and milk and add melted butter. Make a well in centre of the dry ingredients and pour in milk and butter. Stir quickly until just combined. Three-quarters fill greased muffin pans and bake at 200°C for 15-20 minutes.

Banana & Date Muffins

Sweet and sticky – yummy!

2½ cups oat-bran
1½ cups wholemeal flour
6 teaspoons baking powder
2 teaspoons mixed spice
1 teaspoon cinnamon
500g finely chopped banana
100g finely chopped dates
½ cup apple juice concentrate
½ cup cold-pressed grapeseed oil
1 cup evaporated milk
3 egg whites

PLACE oat-bran in a bowl. Add sifted wholemeal flour, baking powder, mixed spice and cinnamon. Distribute flour and spices through oat-bran with hands. Add bananas and dates and toss well to break up and coat with flour. Combine apple juice concentrate, oil and milk, and stir into flour and oat mixture. Beat egg whites until soft, and gently fold through the mixture. Three-quarters fill greased muffin pans and bake at 180°C for 25-30 minutes.

SWEET MUFFINS

Banana & Walnut Muffins

Try walking past these when they're cooling on the rack.

1½ cups flour
1½ teaspoons baking powder
¼ teaspoon nutmeg
¼ cup sugar
½ teaspoon salt
2 bananas, mashed
25g butter, melted
¾ cup milk
1 egg
2 tablespoons oil
½ cup chopped walnuts
½ teaspoon grated orange rind
½ teaspoon grated lemon rind

SIFT flour, baking powder, nutmeg, sugar and salt. Mash bananas and add melted butter, milk, egg, oil, chopped nuts, and orange and lemon rind. Make a well in centre of dry ingredients and gently stir in banana mixture. Three-quarters fill greased muffin pans and bake at 200°C for 15-20 minutes.

Best Banana Muffins

A classic taste sensation.

$1/2$ cup sugar
5 tablespoons vegetable oil
1 cup ripe mashed banana
1 egg, lightly beaten
1 teaspoon vanilla
$1/2$ cup All-bran
$1/2$ cup flour
$1/2$ cup wholemeal flour
$1 1/2$ teaspoons baking powder
$1/4$ teaspoon salt
$1/2$ cup raisins

COMBINE sugar, oil, banana, lightly beaten egg, vanilla and All-bran. Let stand for five minutes. Sift flour, wholemeal flour, baking powder and salt, and add to All-bran mixture. Stir until just combined. Fold in raisins. Three-quarters fill greased muffin pans and bake at 180ºC for 20-25 minutes until golden brown.

SWEET MUFFINS

Blueberry Muffins

Try some other berry fruit for variation on this beauty.

125g butter, melted
2¾ cups flour
1 teaspoon salt
4 teaspoons baking powder
¾ cup castor sugar
4 eggs
1 cup milk
2 cups blueberries, fresh or frozen
extra castor sugar

MELT butter and cool. Sift flour, salt, baking powder and sugar. Beat eggs until thick and fluffy. Whisk in milk and melted butter. Add egg mixture to dry ingredients, then fold in blueberries. Stir to just combine. Three-quarters fill greased muffin pans and sprinkle with castor sugar. Bake at 200°C for about 15 minutes.

From left: Bacon & Tomato Muffins p9; Savoury Cottage Cheese Muffins p20

From left: Carrot Muffins p12; Chilli Corn Muffins p18

From left: Zucchini & Wheatgerm Muffins p22; Cheese & Lentil Muffins p14

From left: Apricot & Lemon Muffins p27;
Cherry & Walnut Muffins p34; Plum Muffins p50

Front left: Kiwifruit Muffins p41; *Right*: Apple, Carrot & Bran Muffins p25

Pineapple Muffins p48

Plum Muffins p50

Front: Strawberry Rhubarb Muffins p53; *Back*: Pistachio Chocolate Muffins p49

Carrot & Ginger Muffins

Spicing up what is already known and loved.

*2 cups flour
1 tablespoon baking powder
1/4 teaspoon ground ginger
1/4 cup brown sugar
3/4 cup grated carrot
1/4 cup crystallized ginger
1 egg
3/4 cup milk
50g butter, melted*

SIFT flour, baking powder and ground ginger. Stir in sugar, carrot and crystallized ginger. Combine egg and milk, and add melted butter. Make a well in centre of dry ingredients and pour in milk and butter. Stir quickly until just mixed. Three-quarters fill greased muffin pans and bake at 200°C for 20 minutes.

SWEET MUFFINS

Cherry & Walnut Muffins

A sweet delight with a bit of crunch.

2 cups flour
1/3 cup castor sugar
3 teaspoons baking powder
1/4 cup chopped glacé cherries
1/3 cup chopped walnuts
1 egg
1 cup milk
1/4 cup butter, melted
1 teaspoon vanilla

SIFT flour, sugar and baking powder, then add cherries and walnuts. Beat together egg, milk, melted butter and vanilla. Add to dry ingredients and mix gently until just combined. Three-quarters fill greased muffin pans and bake at 200°C for 15-20 minutes.

Chocolate & Nutmeg Muffins

Who can resist anything with chocolate in it?

2 cups flour
1 tablespoon baking powder
1/4 teaspoon nutmeg
1/2 cup brown sugar
1 egg
1 1/4 cups milk
50g butter, melted
100g roughly chopped chocolate pieces

SIFT flour, baking powder and nutmeg, and stir in sugar. Mix egg and milk together. Melt butter. Make a well in the dry ingredients and pour in milk and butter. Add chocolate pieces and stir quickly until just combined. Three-quarters fill greased muffin pans and bake at 200°C for 15-20 minutes or until firm.

SWEET MUFFINS

Cranberry & Pecan Muffins

Moist berry flavour with the pleasure of pecan nuts.

1½ cups milk
2 eggs
75g butter, melted
1 cup wholemeal flour
1 cup flour
⅓ cup sugar
3 teaspoons baking powder
½ teaspoon salt
1¼ cups cranberry sauce
100g chopped pecan nuts

COMBINE milk, eggs and melted butter. Beat briskly. Add remaining ingredients and stir until just combined. The batter should look lumpy. Three-quarters fill greased muffin pans and bake at 200°C for 20-25 minutes or until lightly browned.

Date Muffins

Sticky and delicious – wash down with lots of hot tea.

2 tablespoons butter
¼ cup brown sugar
2 eggs
1 cup milk
2 cups flour
1 teaspoon baking powder
pinch of salt
1 cup finely chopped dates

CREAM butter and sugar. Add eggs and milk, then sifted flour, baking powder and salt. Fold in finely chopped dates. Stir to just combine. Three-quarters fill greased muffin pans and bake at 200ºC for 12-15 minutes.

SWEET MUFFINS

Date & Orange Muffins

Tangy orange combines perfectly with the sweet date flavour.

1 orange, peeled and quartered
$1/2$ cup orange juice
1 egg
100g butter, melted
$1 1/2$ cups flour
1 teaspoon baking powder
$1/4$ teaspoon salt
1 teaspoon baking soda
$3/4$ cup sugar
$1/2$ cup chopped dates

REMOVE orange pips and place in food processor. Process until pulp. Add orange juice, egg and melted butter, and combine. Sift flour, baking powder, salt, baking soda and sugar. Add mixture from processor to dry ingredients. Add chopped dates and mix until just combined. Three-quarters fill greased muffin pans and bake at 190°C for 15 minutes or until cooked.

Fruity Bran Muffins

Cook them up and get a friend around for a chat.

1¼ cups All-bran
¾ cup skim milk
1 egg
¼ cup cooking oil
¼ cup raw sugar
1¾ cups self-raising flour
1 teaspoon cinnamon
⅔ cup mixed dried fruit
1 egg white
extra All-bran for topping

PLACE All-bran and skim milk in a bowl and let stand for five minutes to soften. Beat egg, oil, and sugar together and add to All-bran. Sift flour and add to All-bran mixture with cinnamon and mixed fruit. Mix until just combined. Do not overmix. Fold in stiffly beaten egg white. Three-quarters fill greased muffin pans and sprinkle each muffin with some extra All-bran. Bake at 190ºC for 25-30 minutes or until cooked.

SWEET MUFFINS

Honey & Date Muffins

Something special for that sweet tooth.

75g butter
½ cup honey
1½ cups chopped dates
2 eggs
¼ cup milk
1½ cups flour
2 teaspoons baking powder

HEAT butter and honey only long enough to melt butter. Stir in chopped dates. Beat eggs with milk. Sift flour and baking powder. Make a well in centre of flour and add honey and egg mixtures. Mix until dry ingredients are just moistened. Three-quarters fill greased muffin pans and bake at 200°C for 15-20 minutes or until cooked.

Kiwifruit Muffins

Captures the delicate flavour of kiwifruit.

3/4 cup white flour
3 teaspoons baking powder
1/2 cup cornmeal
1/2 cup wholemeal flour
1/2 cup sugar
2 eggs
1/2 cup oil
1/2 cup milk
1/2 cup peeled and chopped kiwifruit

SIFT flour and baking powder. Add cornmeal, wholemeal flour and sugar. Beat eggs, oil and milk, and add to mixture. Fold in chopped kiwifruit and stir until just combined. Three-quarters fill greased muffin pans and bake at 200°C for 15-20 minutes.

SWEET MUFFINS

Lemon Coconut Muffins

A tropical treat.

1 cup All-bran
1½ cups skim milk
1 egg, lightly beaten
2 tablespoons cooking oil
grated rind and juice of 1 lemon
1½ cups self-raising flour
¼ cup castor sugar
½ cup coconut
extra coconut for topping

PLACE All-bran and milk in a large bowl and let stand for five minutes until softened. Stir in lightly beaten egg, oil, lemon rind and juice. Combine flour, sugar and coconut and stir into All-bran mixture. Mix carefully to just combine. Three-quarters fill greased muffin pans and sprinkle with extra coconut. Bake at 190ºC for 25-30 minutes.

Nutty Walnut Muffins

Walnut lovers can't go past these.

100g butter
¼ cup golden syrup
150ml milk
1 cup wholemeal flour
½ cup flour
1 teaspoon baking powder
½ cup baking bran
½ cup wheatgerm
½ cup raw sugar
¼ cup chopped walnuts
1 teaspoon baking soda
¼ cup milk

PUT butter and golden syrup into a small saucepan and heat until butter has melted. Add first measure of milk to saucepan and heat to boiling point. Set aside. Sift flours and baking powder. Add bran, wheatgerm, sugar and walnuts. Mix to just combine. Dissolve baking soda in second measure of milk. Pour milk mixture and first measure of milk onto dry ingredients. Mix lightly until all ingredients are just combined. Three-quarters fill greased muffin pans and bake at 180ºC for 20 minutes.

SWEET MUFFINS

Oat & Orange Muffins

A healthy package with added fruit and nuts.

1 orange, peeled and quartered
2 cups oat-bran
¼ cup raw sugar
1 teaspoon mixed spice
2 teaspoons baking powder
¾ cup sultanas
¼ cup wheatgerm
2 tablespoons vegetable oil
¾ cup milk
1 teaspoon baking soda
¼ cup chopped walnuts for topping

REMOVE orange pips and place orange in food processor. Process until finely chopped. In a mixing bowl, combine oat-bran, raw sugar, mixed spice, baking powder, sultanas and wheatgerm. Heat oil and milk slightly and dissolve baking soda in milk mixture. Add oat-bran mixture and milk to orange in the food processor. Pulse to just combine. Three-quarters fill greased muffin pans, sprinkle with walnuts and bake at 190ºC for 15 minutes or until cooked.

Oaty Apple Walnut Muffins

A winter special – all the good things in one package.

100g butter
2 teaspoons grated lemon rind
¾ cup brown sugar
1 egg
1 cup self-raising flour
½ teaspoon cinnamon
¼ teaspoon baking soda
¼ teaspoon salt
¾ cup unsweetened stewed apples
1 cup quick-cooking rolled oats
½ cup sultanas
½ cup chopped walnuts

CREAM butter, lemon rind and sugar. Add egg and beat well. Sift flour, cinnamon, baking soda and salt, and add alternately to the creamed mixture with stewed apples. Fold in oats, sultanas and walnuts. Three-quarters fill greased muffin pans and bake at 180°C for 20-25 minutes.

SWEET MUFFINS

Orange Marmalade Muffins

A tangy, delicious morning tea muffin.

1½ cups self-raising flour
1¼ cups All-bran
½ cup chopped walnuts
1 egg
grated rind and juice of 1 orange
½ cup marmalade
¼ cup skim milk
¼ cup oil

Sugar 'n' Spice Topping
2 tablespoons brown sugar
2 tablespoons castor sugar
¼ teaspoon cinnamon
ground nutmeg to taste
¼ cup plain flour
shredded orange rind
1½ tablespoons butter

COMBINE flour, All-bran and walnuts in a large bowl. Beat egg, orange rind and juice, marmalade, skim milk and oil. Add to dry ingredients and mix until just combined. For the topping, combine all the dry ingredients and orange rind. Rub in the butter until mixture resembles breadcrumbs. Three-quarters fill greased muffin pans and sprinkle each muffin with a little of the topping. Bake at 200ºC for 20 minutes.

Orange Nut Muffins

A thrilling fruit and nut combination.

1 cup plain flour
$1/3$ cup sugar
$1^1/_2$ teaspoons baking powder
$1/4$ teaspoon salt
$1^1/_2$ cups All-bran
$1/3$ cup chopped walnuts
1 egg
2 teaspoons grated orange rind
$2/3$ cup orange juice
$1/3$ cup orange marmalade
$1/4$ cup skim milk
$1/4$ cup cooking oil

COMBINE flour, sugar, baking powder, salt, All-bran and walnuts. Make a well in the centre. Combine egg, orange rind, orange juice, marmalade, skim milk and oil. Add to dry ingredients and blend until just combined. Three-quarters fill greased muffin pans and bake at 200ºC for 20-25 minutes.

Pineapple Muffins

Lovely tropical flavour that goes well with fresh coffee.

2 cups flour
1 teaspoon baking powder
1 cup sugar
1 teaspoon salt
1 egg
1 cup milk
1 tablespoon butter, melted
$1/2$ cup drained, crushed pineapple

SIFT dry ingredients. Beat egg with milk, and add butter and pineapple. Make a well in the centre of dry ingredients, add liquid and stir until just damp and lumpy. Three-quarters fill greased muffin pans and bake at 200ºC for 15-20 minutes.

Pistachio Chocolate Muffins

A real treat for chocolate lovers.

1/3 cup butter
2 cups flour
3 teaspoons baking powder
1 teaspoon salt
1/3 cup sugar
2 eggs
1 cup milk
2 teaspoons rum
1/2 cup chopped pistachio nuts
1/2 cup chocolate bits
1/3 cup finely chopped pistachio nuts

RUB butter into flour, baking powder and salt. Add sugar. Beat eggs, milk and rum. Make a well in centre of dry ingredients and add milk mixture, chopped nuts and chocolate bits. Mix very lightly until just combined. Three-quarters fill greased muffin pans and sprinkle with finely chopped pistachio nuts. Bake at 200°C for 20-25 minutes.

SWEET MUFFINS

Plum Muffins

Tangy, fresh flavour – highly recommended.

10 to 12 dark ripe plums
3 cups flour
1 tablespoon baking powder
¾ cup sugar
1 tablespoon grated lemon rind
50g butter, melted
2 eggs, lightly beaten
1¼ cups milk
extra 2 tablespoons sugar

PEEL and stone plums, and roughly chop flesh. Set aside. Sift flour and baking powder and stir in the first measure of sugar and lemon rind. Combine melted butter and lightly beaten eggs, and add milk. Add milk mixture to flour and gently stir to just moisten. Fold in chopped plums. Three-quarters fill greased muffin pans. Sprinkle with extra sugar. Bake at 200°C for 15-20 minutes.

Pumpkin & Chocolate Chip Muffins

A melt-in-the-mouth muffin.

1 cup sliced almonds
1³/₄ cups flour
1 teaspoon allspice
1 teaspoon garam masala
¹/₄ teaspoon baking powder
1 teaspoon baking soda
¹/₄ teaspoon salt
1 cup sugar
2 eggs
1 cup cooked mashed pumpkin
150g butter, melted
1 cup chocolate chips

PLACE almonds on oven tray and bake at 180°C for about five minutes or until lightly browned. Sift flour, allspice, garam masala, baking powder, baking soda and salt. Add sugar. In a separate bowl, beat eggs and add pumpkin and melted butter. Beat to combine. Fold in almonds and chocolate chips. Quickly fold in dry ingredients. Three-quarters fill greased muffin pans and bake at 180°C for 20 minutes or until cooked.

SWEET MUFFINS

Raisin Muffins

Another old favourite that is hard to resist.

1½ cups wholemeal flour
⅓ cup brown sugar
3 teaspoons baking powder
½ teaspoon salt
1 teaspoon cinnamon
½ cup wheatgerm
¾ cup raisins
⅔ cup milk
⅓ cup oil
2 eggs, lightly beaten

SIFT flour adding any husks in sifter to the bowl. Mix in sugar, baking powder, salt, cinnamon, wheatgerm and raisins. Combine milk, oil and lightly beaten eggs. Add to dry ingredients and mix until just moistened. Three-quarters fill greased muffin pans and bake at 200°C for 20 minutes.

Strawberry Rhubarb Muffins

You can also try other berry fruit in this tasty recipe.

1 cup rolled oats
1 cup strawberry yoghurt
125g butter, melted
½ cup brown sugar
1 egg
1 cup flour
½ teaspoon salt
1 teaspoon baking powder
½ teaspoon baking soda
1 teaspoon cinnamon
¾ cup bran
¾ cup finely chopped rhubarb
6 tablespoons strawberry jam

SOAK rolled oats in strawberry yoghurt for five minutes. Stir melted butter and brown sugar into yoghurt. Lightly beat egg and add to yoghurt mixture. Sift flour, salt, baking powder, baking soda and cinnamon and add with bran to yoghurt mixture. Stir until dry ingredients are just moistened. Fold in chopped rhubarb and strawberry jam. Three-quarters fill greased muffin pans and bake at 190ºC for 18-20 minutes.

Sultana Sesame Muffins

The sesame seeds add a real zing.

2 cups flour
¼ cup sugar
4 teaspoons baking powder
1 teaspoon salt (optional)
½ teaspoon ginger
¼ teaspoon cinnamon
¾ cup chopped sultanas
1 egg
1 cup milk
⅓ cup butter, melted
1 tablespoon sesame seeds
1 tablespoon brown sugar
pinch of ginger

SIFT flour, sugar, baking powder, salt, first measure of ginger and cinnamon. Add sultanas and mix well. In a small bowl, beat egg and add milk and melted butter. Stir into flour mixture only until just combined. Three-quarters fill greased muffin pans. Combine sesame seeds, brown sugar and pinch of ginger and sprinkle over muffins. Bake at 220°C for 20-25 minutes.

Sweet Sherry Currant Muffins

A hint of Christmas pudding – try with custard.

½ cup currants
2 tablespoons sweet sherry
100g butter, softened
½ cup packed brown sugar
2 eggs
2 cups plain flour
3 teaspoons baking powder
½ teaspoon baking soda
½ teaspoon salt
1¼ cups buttermilk (or soured milk)
2 tablespoons castor sugar
1 teaspoon cinnamon

SOAK currants in sherry until plump. Beat softened butter and brown sugar until fluffy. Beat in eggs then stir in currants. Sift flour, baking powder, baking soda and salt, and fold into creamed mixture alternately with buttermilk. Mix until just combined. Three-quarters fill greased muffin pans. Combine castor sugar and cinnamon and sprinkle over muffins.
Bake at 200ºC for 15 minutes until browned.

SWEET MUFFINS

Yoghurt & Sultana Muffins

A lovely moist, fruity muffin.

1 cup plain flour
½ teaspoon baking powder
½ teaspoon salt
¼ teaspoon baking soda
¾ cup wheatgerm
4 tablespoons packed brown sugar
1 egg, beaten
1 cup yoghurt
1 tablespoon milk (optional)
75g melted butter, cooled
½ cup sultanas

SIFT flour, baking powder, salt and baking soda. Stir in wheatgerm and brown sugar. Combine beaten egg, yoghurt (adding milk if very thick) and cooled butter, and add to dry ingredients. Add sultanas and stir until just moistened. Three-quarters fill greased muffin pans and bake at 190°C for 30-35 minutes.

Cardamon Muffins

A savoury muffin with a touch of Indian spice.

1½ cups self-raising flour
pinch salt
1 teaspoon ground cardamon
¼ cup sugar
1 egg
50g butter, melted
⅓ cup sour cream

SIFT flour, salt and cardamon, and stir in sugar. Beat egg, melted butter and sour cream. Pour onto dry ingredients and mix until just combined. Three-quarters fill greased muffin pans and bake at 200ºC for 15-20 minutes.

SPICY MUFFINS

Cinnamon Apple Muffins

Another old favourite and great with your morning coffee.

60g butter, melted
1/2 cup sugar
1 large egg, beaten
1/2 cup milk
1 1/2 cups flour
1 tablespoon baking powder
1/2 teaspoon cinnamon
1/2 teaspoon salt
1 cup freshly grated apple

Topping
1/4 cup sugar
1/4 cup chopped walnuts
1/2 teaspoon cinnamon

IN a large bowl, combine melted butter, sugar, beaten egg and milk. Sift flour, baking powder, cinnamon and salt. Add to butter mixture and stir until just combined. The batter should look lumpy. Fold in freshly grated apple. Three-quarters fill greased muffin pans and sprinkle combined topping over muffins. Bake at 180°C for 15-20 minutes.

Ginger Muffins

A refreshing taste – a real breakfast treat.

1 cup milk
50g butter
1 tablespoon golden syrup
1 teaspoon baking soda
1 egg
1 cup oat-bran
½ cup sugar
2 tablespoons chopped crystallized ginger
1 teaspoon ground ginger
1 cup flour
½ cup rolled oats
½ teaspoon salt

HEAT milk, butter and golden syrup until butter melts. Add baking soda and egg. In a bowl, mix oat-bran, sugar, crystallized and ground ginger, flour, rolled oats and salt. Add the milk mixture and mix until only just combined. Three-quarters fill greased muffin pans and bake at 200ºC for 10-15 minutes.

Spicy All-Bran Muffins

Healthy and tasty – what more could you ask for.

1¼ cups All-bran
1½ cups skim milk
1 egg yolk
60g butter, melted
½ cup chopped raisins or dates
1½ cups self-raising flour
1 teaspoon cinnamon
½ teaspoon nutmeg
¼ cup castor sugar
2 egg whites, stiffly beaten
extra All-bran for topping

PLACE All-bran and milk in a large bowl and let stand for five minutes until softened. Beat in egg yolk, melted butter and raisins. Sift flour and spices. Stir in sugar and add to All-bran mixture. Fold in stiffly beaten egg whites. Three-quarters fill greased muffin pans and sprinkle with extra All-bran. Bake at 200ºC for 25-30 minutes.

Spicy Fruit Muffins

A great alternative when hot cross buns are hard to get.

50g butter
½ cup sugar
1 egg
1 grated apple
½ teaspoon baking soda
1 dessertspoon boiling water
¾ cup flour
½ teaspoon cinnamon
½ teaspoon mixed spice
¼ cup sultanas

CREAM butter and sugar. Add egg and beat well. Stir in grated apple, soda dissolved in water, flour and spices. Mix lightly then fold in sultanas. Three-quarters fill greased muffin pans and bake at 200ºC for 15 minutes or until firm.

Wholemeal Spicy Pumpkin Muffins

Especially for lovers of pumpkin pie.

½ cup packed brown sugar
¼ cup vegetable oil
1 egg
½ cup mashed cooked pumpkin
½ cup sultanas
1½ cups wholemeal self-raising flour
½ teaspoon salt
¼ teaspoon nutmeg
¼ teaspoon mixed spice
½ cup milk (approx.)

BEAT together sugar, oil, egg and mashed pumpkin until well blended. Stir in sultanas. Sift flour, salt and spices. Stir into pumpkin mixture alternately with milk until just combined. Three-quarters fill greased muffin pans and bake at 200°C for 15-20 minutes.

Index

Almond Chip	23
Apple	24
Apple, Carrot & Bran	25
Apple, Date & Bran	26
Apricot & Lemon	27
Apricot & Walnut	28
Bacon & Cheese	8
Bacon & Tomato	9
Banana & Date	29
Banana & Walnut	30
Bean Sprout & Cottage Cheese	10
Best Banana	31
Blueberry	32
Caraway & Cheese	11
Cardamon	57
Carrot	12
Carrot & Ginger	33
Cheese	13
Cheese & Lentil	14
Cheese & Onion	15
Cheesy Sunflower Seed	16
Cherry & Walnut	34
Chicken & Curry	17
Chilli Corn	18
Chocolate & Nutmeg	35
Cinnamon Apple	58
Corn & Pecan	19
Cranberry & Pecan	36
Date	37
Date & Orange	38
Fruity Bran	39
Ginger	59
Honey & Date	40
Kiwifruit	41
Lemon Coconut	42
Nutty Walnut	43
Oat & Orange	44
Oaty Apple Walnut	45

Orange Marmalade..........................46
Orange Nut.......................................47
Pineapple..48
Pistachio Chocolate........................49
Plum..50
Pumpkin & Chocolate Chip.............51
Raisin..52
Savoury Cottage Cheese..................20
Spicy All-Bran..................................60
Spicy Fruit..61
Strawberry Rhubarb.........................53
Sultana Sesame................................54
Sweet Sherry Currant.......................55
Wholemeal.......................................21
Wholemeal Spicy Pumpkin.............62
Yoghurt & Sultana............................56
Zucchini & Wheatgerm....................22